God's Power Through the Laying On of Hands

by
Norvel Hayes

Unless otherwise indicated,
all Scripture quotations are taken from
the *King James Version* of the Bible.

FOREWORD

Norvel Hayes is one of the most unique persons we have ever met! His faith and beliefs are so strong they splash over on every person he meets. There are times when his grammar is unbelievable, but the message is believable, because it is right in line with the Bible, as he has become one of the most unusual and outstanding Bible teachers in the world today.

He is a successful businessman who operates some eight businesses along with relentlessly carrying out the burning desire of his life, which is to share the gospel in its entirety.

He has a compelling drive to share the total Great Commission with the Christian world, and this book shares the last part, ". . . they shall lay hands on the sick, and they shall recover."

If you've never laid hands on anyone, you will want to after you read this book, and if you've never had hands laid on you, you will want to have this done when you hear the simple teaching on the laying on of hands.

He is sometimes blunt in his comments, but his purpose is to make all of us take another look at what the Bible really says.

This is one of the exciting messages he presents in his seminars . . . and signs and wonders follow!

Charles and Frances Hunter

TABLE OF CONTENTS

CHAPTER ONE

GOD'S POWER IN YOUR HANDS

What were the last eleven words that came out of Jesus Christ's mouth on the earth, right before he left the earth and went straight up through the air into heaven?

He said, *"They shall lay hands on the sick, and they shall recover."*

That means get well, not be sick anymore, be healed!

God releases his power through the laying on of hands.

I will explain to you in this book and show you chapter and verse that the laying on of hands is for the church today. When I say the church, I mean Baptists, Methodists, Catholics, Presbyterians, Lutherans, Assembly of God, Church of God, Church of the Brethren, Church of Christ — I mean anybody's church. Those names are just names that have been made up by men. Those names are not in the Bible, but if they choose to name their church those names, that's up to them. God only requires people to believe the Bible. God's power works for everybody the same if they believe his word. On the subject of laying on of hands, Jesus Christ himself said, "They shall lay hands on the sick and they shall recover." Knowing that Jesus is one who cannot lie, then you can plainly see that it is our duty as believers, regardless of what church we may go to, to do as Jesus says.

DO YOU DO IT?

If you don't lay hands on the sick, but you are a believer in the Lord Jesus Christ, and if you have sense enough to read, can you see that you are disobeying the Lord Jesus Christ? Jesus says that if you believe in him, YOU will lay hands on the sick, and YOU will see them recover.

Now Jesus is really saying to you, if you are willing to work for me, and you will go visit the sick, and lay your hands on them, then I promise you that my Father's mighty power will come through YOUR hands and go into the sick person's body; that power that God releases to come through YOUR hands and go into their bodies will just dissolve the sickness and the disease that is causing that person torment, and pain, and heartaches, and causing trouble, and costing money that they could be giving to spread the gospel. Now if you do lay hands on the sick already, then you are doing what Jesus told you to do. And you will definitely see sick people healed right before your very eyes by merely believing and laying your hands on them. God's power will come through YOUR hands.

As long as I attended the First Baptist Church, God's power never came through my hands, because I never laid my hands on anyone. I had no earthly idea that God's power would work through my hands and that sick people could be healed. My brother and sister, it is a long, long way from the First Baptist Church to watching cripples walk out of their wheel chairs! But I promise you that Jesus himself cannot lie. I am a living example of the truth of what Jesus can do through anyone who will only believe. He can do it even in a First Baptist Church!

I received a phone call several months ago from the Reverend Ken Sumrall, a Southern Baptist pastor. He went to a Southern Baptist seminary. He has built a great Bible college in Pensacola, Florida, called Liberty Bible

College, a beautiful and wonderful place for young people to be trained in the Bible. I met Rev. Ken Sumrall a
couple of times over the years. I had never visited his
Bible school, but I had heard a lot of good reports from
the people who went to school there. He called and asked
me to be one of the speakers at his convention for the
Bible school which he held once a year on the campus. I
had the dates open, and I agreed to go. We had a great
time with services in the morning and at night also.

The last day of that wonderful convention, on a
Sunday morning, after I finished speaking, I began to
pray for the people. I noticed over to my left that there
was one lady on a stretcher who had been brought in, and
two other ladies sitting in wheel chairs. I walked over and
laid my hands on the lady on the stretcher and the Spirit
of the Lord came upon her. But it seemed she put no
effort of her own with God's power to jump off the
stretcher. I walked over to one of the people in the wheel
chair and laid my hands on her, and she just sat there. I
walked over to the other lady in the wheel chair and laid
my hands on her. She began to stretch out her legs and
jump forth, and she walked right out of the wheel chair!
The legs she stretched out became strong within a matter
of ten seconds after I laid my hands on her. God's power
came upon her, and she yielded herself to that power and
began to give action and began to believe. She walked off
right out from under my hands. She pushed her wheel
chair all around the church. She would stop every few
steps and raise her hands and praise the Lord. They took
her back to the nursing home. And if you can imagine,
the people in the nursing home came out of their rooms
and said, "What's happened to you?" She told them,
"God healed me this morning, and I walked out of the
wheel chair." This caused quite a bit of excitement in the
nursing home.

At the evening service, her nurse came with her to the
service and came up behind the pulpit and gave testimony

about how she had been taking care of the lady and that the woman was a cerebral palsy case. She was told that she would never walk again, but by the laying on of hands, God's power went into her body, and she walked off.

The other wheel chair case may be healed by now or she may not be. The lady on the stretcher may be healed by now, or she may be dead. I have been in many cities since that time, but if the other two women would have believed that they were healed that day in Pensacola, Florida when I laid my hands on them, then both of the ladies would be well today and normal. Now the reason I can say that is because I laid my hands on them, and God's power went through them. The reason I laid my hands on them is because Jesus said, "They shall lay hands on the sick, and they shall recover" (Mark 16:18).

Many church people wonder why Jesus doesn't heal the sick people in their church today. Some say to me, "I've never seen a crippled person walk out of a wheel chair at our church." I always ask them, "Do your people lay hands on the sick in Jesus' name?" And, of course, they say, "No." So I say, "Well, Jesus gave it as a duty to believers." That automatically makes it available for the church — anybody's church.

God doesn't have the sixteenth chapter of the book of Mark in the Bible just for a few Pentecostal people. It's in there for everyone. All the First Baptist pastors in the world are supposed to be laying hands on sick people; and if they would, God's power would work with them, confirming the word with signs following.

Always remember this, God's power works with the Bible. He tells us in the Bible the way he does things; and that's the ONLY way he does things. You must learn that if you say you are a believer in the Lord Jesus Christ, you must obey him. Jesus said if you love him to keep his commandments (John 14:23). You must obey Jesus and not men. Men will always tell you what THEY think, and what THEY believe and what THEY do and where THEY go to church, or I believe this and I don't believe that. But you see, what men believe or don't believe isn't worth fifteen cents to Jesus. It is what the Bible says that counts. Nowhere in the Bible will you find Jesus saying that he would go with the Methodists and confirm what they believe, or the Catholics or the Pentecostals or any other group. No, the Bible says in Mark 16, verse 20, "And they went forth, and preached every where, the Lord working with them, and confirming the word with signs following."

God will go with you, but he will only confirm chapter and verse for what you say you believe.

And stop trying to figure God out.

Just read and believe what you read. Jesus Christ is one who can be trusted. You don't have to wonder if he is telling you the truth.

CHAPTER TWO

LAYING ON OF HANDS IS A DOCTRINE OF THE CHURCH

Let us study together the sixteenth chapter of the book of Mark, beginning at verse 15. Many churches refer to this passage as the Great Commission that Jesus gave to believers, and I believe this also. That verse says, "And he said unto them, Go ye into all the world, and preach the gospel to every creature." That means everybody, everywhere. God loves everyone the same, and God is not willing for even one person to ever perish (2 Peter 3:9 and John 3:16).

Let's continue with verse 16, "He that believeth and is baptized shall be saved . . ." Being baptized is one of the doctrines of the New Testament Church, and most churches practice this doctrine. Jesus continues, "But he that believeth not shall be damned." There is no hope for people who won't believe. Whatever you can believe God for, you can have. What you don't believe God for, you can't have.

"And these signs shall follow them that believe . . ." (vs. 17). Jesus is saying here that if you believe in him that he has some orders for you, and if you will carry out these orders, victory will be yours.

The first sign that follows them that believe: "In my name shall they cast out devils . . ." Do you do that? If you don't cast out devils in Jesus' name, why don't you?

Let's look at the next order Jesus gave as a sign of a believer. "They shall speak with new tongues . . ." Do you speak with new tongues? You can learn in detail in the fourteenth chapter of the book of First Corinthians how important that is for the church and for believers. It builds you up in God to speak with new tongues (Jude 20). You should have a prayer language so that the Spirit can speak through you (Romans 8:26 and 27). The Bible says that every believer can sing in his own understanding and sing in the spirit (I Cor. 14:15). The Bible says that every believer can pray in his own understanding and can pray in the spirit also (I Cor. 14:15 and Ephesians 6:18). You have to obey and believe ALL that Jesus said — not just a part — in order to get the results he said you would get. The power to heal or do miracles comes from the receiving of power the same way the disciples did in the Bible. They all spoke in tongues when they received power. If we do like the Bible says, it works. If we skip part of Jesus' command, it won't work.

Verse 18 in Mark continues, "They shall take up serpents; and if they drink any deadly thing, it shall not hurt them . . ."

Paul took up a serpent as recorded in the book of Acts, chapter 28, verse 3, and in verse 5 the Bible says, "And he shook off the beast into the fire, and felt no harm." And it will not hurt you! In the great book, LIKE A MIGHTY WIND, by Mel Tari, they drank deadly poison on a mission trip because the chief of the tribe was trying to kill them. They drank the deadly poison, and it did not hurt them.

Notice the last commission Jesus has for the believer. Remember, you are studying the last words that came from the lips of the Lord Jesus Christ while he was on earth. These are orders he has given to believers, not just to people who hold a high office in the church, although these orders apply to them also. These are orders to ALL believers. The last part of verse 18 of chapter 16 of the book of Mark says, "They shall lay hands on the sick, and they shall recover." I can't emphasize enough that these are the last eleven words that Jesus said on earth: "They shall lay hands on the sick, and they shall recover."

Men and their beliefs need to be questioned. It is our responsibility to check up on men — to search the scriptures (Acts 17:11) and see if what they are teaching us is what the Bible says. Some men want to teach you things from their heads and not from the Bible. You need to understand that the devil talks to your head. The devil uses the power of thought suggestion. Jesus says one thing, and the devil will tell you something else.

The people are the church. Believers are supposed to obey the head of the church, the Lord Jesus Christ, not men or ideas planted in men's minds by the devil. The Lord Jesus Christ came to earth, died on the cross, arose again on the third day and appeared to quite a number of people. Then he went back to heaven and is now sitting at the right hand of God. Jesus is the head of the church (Eph. 1:22). Pastors of the local churches are the under-shepherds (Acts 20:28). Jesus is "The Good Shepherd" (John 10:14). The pastor of a flock is supposed to take his orders from the Good Shepherd, the Lord Jesus Christ. One order Jesus gave is to lay hands on the sick, and know they shall recover.

I would like to bring to your attention at this time something that could literally bind you and cause you not to receive this lesson from God in heaven. The blessings of God will not come from heaven through the doctrines of men. They only flow through the doctrines of the church.

Notice in the book of Matthew chapter 15 that God is speaking, telling you and warning you that many people on earth say with their mouth that they worship him, and they honor him, and they honor him with their lips, but God says, "In vain they do worship me, teaching for doctrines the commandments of men" (vs. 9). You are not supposed to have any commandments or doctrines of men. Every doctrine that is not scriptural is a doctrine of a man. Jesus said to lay hands on the sick, and they shall recover. If a man comes along and says, "I am a local shepherd of a certain-certain flock, and we will pray for the sick the way that I see fit, and I don't think it is necessary to lay hands on the sick . . ." he is establishing the doctrine of a man. And the blessings of God to heal the sick will not come to that man or to his certain-certain flock.

Sometimes people look at me strangely when I ask them, "Can you read?"

"Oh, yes, I can read," they say.

I ask them, "Do you know what your hands are?" Then they really look at me funny. I used to hold my hands up in front of them and wave them just a little bit and say, "These two things down here at the ends of your arms — you are supposed to pick them up and lay them on sick people because Jesus says they will recover if you do." I'll say, "Why don't you do that?"

"Well," they say, "that's not the way we do it at our church."

And I say, "Well, you have a doctrine and a commandment of a man. Jesus knew what he was talking about, and you just better listen to him. JESUS CANNOT LIE."

What happens when you accept a doctrine or commandment of a man? Matthew 15 says, "Thus have ye made the commandment of God of none effect by your tradition" (vs. 6). People tell me all over America, "Well, I've gone to this church all my life and all my friends go there, and this is the way WE do it." It really doesn't make any difference the way YOU do it. If you don't do it the way God says to do it, you won't ever receive anything from God. You either obey the Lord Jesus Christ, and the word of God, or you get over into the commandments and doctrines of men. And God just doesn't work through the commandments and doctrines of men.

A doctrine of the church is very important. In John 14 Jesus says that if you love him, you will keep HIS commandments (vs. 15). That means obey the Bible, not the commandments of men. Obey the doctrines of the New Testament. All right, if you would like to know the principles of the doctrines of Christ, you can find them in Hebrews, chapter 6, verses 1 and 2. You will find in those two verses the doctrines that Jesus taught, namely: repentance, faith, baptisms, laying on of hands, resurrection and judgment. You must learn these first principles, Jesus says, before you can go on to the other things in the Bible. In Hebrews 5 we are shown the need to be taught these doctrines, "For when for the time ye ought to be teachers, ye have need that one teach you again which be the first principles of the oracles of God ..." (vs. 12). Jesus is telling us that we should stick to his doctrines; he is having me teach you again what the doctrines are that he expects the church to follow.

The church has developed many other doctrines over the years. Many local assemblies, however, obey some of these doctrines of Jesus. Most all churches in the world believe that you must have faith, and that is a doctrine of Christ. Almost any church believes you should be baptized in water, and that is one of the correct baptisms Jesus taught. But the one we are studying is the doctrine of the laying on of hands, and many churches do not have this doctrine of Christ included in their teachings. The minds of men have taken it out of the local church, and they do not practice it. That is the reason that God doesn't approve of that part of their teachings, and that is why they don't see any sick people healed at their church. These churches do many things right and according to the Bible. If they would just add the doctrine of Christ of laying on of hands, because Jesus told them to, they could begin to watch their sick people be healed and their cripples walk off.

Let me give you a warning about any doctrine that cannot give a chapter and verse for it. The Bible warns you of those types of people. In 2 John, verses 9 and 10, we are told, "Whosoever transgresseth, and abideth not in the doctrine of Christ, hath not God. He that abideth in the doctrine of Christ, he hath both the Father and the Son. If there come any unto you, and bring not THIS DOCTRINE, (in other words, the doctrine of Christ) receive him not into your house, (or your church; they had church in the house in those days) neither bid him God speed."

First Timothy 4 warns, "Now the Spirit speaketh expressly, that in the latter times (that's now) some shall depart from the faith, giving heed to seducing spirits, and doctrines of devils" (vs. 1). Now that's really saying the doctrines of men's minds, because the devil uses the supernatural power of thought suggestion which speaks to men's minds to get them to not believe the Bible and obey it the way it is written. The devil tells a man's mind that it's okay to do things the way he wants to. The devil will say, "You're the boss here, do it the way you think best." He will say, "It really doesn't matter what the Bible says. Some things in the Bible aren't for today, anyway, and besides, things have changed, and a lot of the stuff in the Bible doesn't apply today." The devil hates man, and he doesn't want to see him get well and recover. The devil wants you to be sick and die. God loves us, and he has set this doctrine of laying on of hands into the church so we may be well and prosper as our soul prospers (3 John 2). He wants us to be sanctified wholly, spirit, soul and body (1 Thess. 5:23). He says in

Exodus 15:26, "I am the Lord that healeth thee." He will release his mighty power to work in and through us as we obey him and lay our hands on people to see them healed.

Now don't let the devil sell you on the idea that because you go to a church that doesn't practice the doctrine of laying on of hands, that God's power wouldn't come through YOUR hands. God's power will flow through your hands — or anybody's hands who is a believer in the Lord Jesus Christ. In 1 Timothy 4, verses 12 and 13, Paul is giving Timothy some instructions as a believer, and these are excellent instructions for us also, "Let no man despise thy youth; but be thou an example of the BELIEVERS, in word, in conversation, in charity, in spirit, in faith, in purity.

"Till I come, give attendance to reading, to exhortation, to DOCTRINE."

We are to be examples of believers in every part of our life. We are to give great attendance to the doctrines of our church. God hasn't put doctrines in the church to be taken out by men. They are rules to go by. Notice verse 14: "Neglect not the gift that is in thee, which was given thee by prophecy, with the laying on of the hands of the presbytery." The gift which he received by the laying on of hands was the Holy Ghost. The Holy Ghost confirms the word with signs following. That's the reason when you lay your hands on somebody, both of you believing, the Spirit of God will begin to work to bring help to that person.

Continuing with verse 15, "Meditate upon these things; give thyself wholly to them . . ." We are supposed to meditate on the things of God, we are supposed to give ourselves wholly to them. Have you meditated upon the doctrine of the laying on of hands? Have you given yourself wholly to it? In other words, do you lay hands on people? Jesus said for you to, if you are a believer. "That thy profiting may appear to all." That's the last part of verse 15. If you will obey the doctrine of the laying on of hands, everybody will profit. The profiting of the doctrine will appear to all. "Take heed unto thyself, and unto the doctrine, continue in them (the doctrines of Christ): for in doing this, thou shalt both save thyself, and them that hear thee" (vs. 16).

Oh, isn't it beautiful! Isn't it wonderful that God would give us such a simple doctrine. It doesn't cost anything. We just lift our hands and lay them on some individual who needs help, and God helps them. Isn't it wonderful that God would do that for the believers in him?

But you can never help anyone nor can you ever receive help for yourself until you make up your mind to obey the doctrine of the laying on of hands. Then you can receive and others can receive from you. "For in doing this thou shalt both save thyself, and them that hear thee."

CHAPTER THREE

TRANSFER OF POWER AND AUTHORITY

I want you to understand that people need to be trained and taught to believe the Bible. You must believe the Bible so you can have the results that are in the Bible. I can show you a hospital full of sick people in most every town in the country. They want to receive healing for their bodies and go home well, but they can't. Most of them don't know of anybody who will come and lay hands on them and pray for them. Most of them don't know they can lay their own hands on their own bodies and pray the prayer of faith and God's power will go through their own hands into their bodies and give them their healing. The scriptures say that the people are destroyed for lack of knowledge (Hosea 4:6).

I want to show you now how God has transferred his power and authority from himself to Jesus to those who believe. You must know that you have the power and authority vested in you as a believer, You must believe God means for YOU to lay hands on the sick. Most of you believe that Jesus healed the sick. So let us study the scriptures together now and see where the power and authority were transferred to you.

Look at John 3, verse 35, "The Father loveth the Son, and hath given all things into his hand." This is just one of many scriptures which show that God gave to Jesus all power and authority. He gave ALL THINGS into his hand.

Into his what?

Into his HAND.

Now verse 36, "He that believeth on (or obeyeth) the Son hath everlasting life: and he that believeth (or obeyeth) not the Son shall not see life; but the wrath of God abideth on him." Notice what the Bible is telling us here. He that believeth not the Son shall not see life. Another way to translate the word "believe" is "obey." So if we obey not Jesus, we will not see life. Jesus said, "Lay hands on the sick, and they shall recover." He that believeth not that, will have to spend his life in sickness and disease. If he believeth not the doctrine of the church, of laying on of hands, he will have to live with his diseases. God's power follows the word in Jesus' name.

Now look at Matthew 10, "And when he had called unto him his twelve disciples, he gave them power (or authority) against unclean spirits, to cast them out, and to heal all manner of sickness and all manner of disease" (vs.1). And Acts 5 says, "And by the HANDS of the apostles were many signs and wonders wrought among the people . . ." (vs. 12), showing that the disciples continued to walk in the power and authority which Jesus gave to them as the church began to be established in the world.

"Well," you say, "that was Jesus, and the apostles. That doesn't happen any more. It won't happen through me." But we have already studied Mark 16, and this chapter gives you the authority. All that Jesus requires of you is to be a believer, and he says the signs and wonders will follow the believers. Believers shall lay hands on the sick, and they shall recover.

Let's look at the same Great Commission as given in Matthew 28, beginning at verse 18, "And Jesus came and spake unto them, saying, All power is given unto me in heaven and in earth." Here again we see that Jesus knew he had been given the power and authority by God. "Go ye therefore, and teach all nations, baptizing them in the name of the Father, and of the Son, and of the Holy Ghost; teaching them to observe all things whatsoever I have commanded you . . ."

Jesus says to teach EVERYTHING he taught. He is telling his disciples to go and teach all nations everything he had taught them. You believe in being baptized in water. Jesus said to be baptized in water. Jesus also said to lay hands on the sick, and they shall recover.

To lay hands on the sick is one of those "all things whatsoever I have commanded you" Jesus is talking about. And what is his final promise if we do all these things? "And, lo, I am with you alway, even unto the end of the world. Amen."

Do you want Jesus to be with you always?

Do you want him to stay with you until the end?

Receive this teaching I am giving you. Jesus has told me to teach you. Now you can also go and teach others, and the church will be stronger and richer and full of health because Jesus is with us and will stay with us until the end. Glory be to God forevermore!

In the Old Testament we see that God had the practice of the laying on of hands many, many centuries ago. He has just brought it on into the New Testament to allow us to continue to receive his blessings right now in the days and minutes in which we live. If we will obey him, his mighty power flows. If we don't, his people suffer, and it isn't God's fault.

In Numbers 8, talking about the Levites, God told Moses to "Bring the Levites before the Lord: and the children of Israel shall put their hands upon the Levites . . . that they may execute the service of the Lord" (vs. 10,11). They were to lay their hands on them.

Did you get that?

Lay their hands on them!

Oh, how wonderful it is! God's mighty power would flow throughout the human race by the laying on of hands. It is so important to God that we lay on hands. Isaiah 55, verse 8 says, "For my thoughts are not your thoughts, neither are your ways my ways, saith the Lord." You see, if we will just do it God's way, we can have all the things that God wants us to have.

Another place that shows how important the laying on of hands is to God can be found in Numbers 27, "And the Lord said unto Moses, Take thee Joshua the son of Nun, a man in whom is the spirit, and lay thine hand upon him . . ." And he laid his hands upon him, and gave him a charge, as the Lord commanded by the hand of Moses" (vss. 18, 23). Here the laying on of hands was so important to God that he had Moses perform this ordinance before all the congregation of the children of Israel. God wanted them to recognize that the power and authority that had been vested in Moses was now transferred to Joshua. The children of Israel were now to follow and obey Joshua. This same power and authority has been transferred to us by Jesus in the Great Commission in Mark 16. We are to lay our hands on people in front of whoever is present, and they shall recover. Jesus wants us as believers to do it today. He is not here on the earth today to do it, so he transferred his power to us. Just as Moses was being replaced by Joshua, so we have taken Jesus' place here on the earth. If we don't do it, the whole church misses the blessing of God.

Why hands? Just because God chose them. It really isn't any of your business why God chooses hands. God could have said, "Put your feet on their stomachs, and I'll heal them." But he didn't. He said, "Lay hands on them," so we lay hands on them because God says to do so, and things happen — great and mighty wonders, signs and healings and miracles, the transferring of God's power and love into people.

Do you do it? If you don't do it, why don't you do it? Jesus told you to.

In the New Testament we have the record of two men whom God called and used mightily, Barnabas and Saul. "As they ministered to the Lord, and fasted, the Holy Ghost said, Separate me Barnabas and Saul for the work whereunto I have called them. And when they had fasted and prayed, and laid their hands on them, they sent them away" (Acts 13: 2, 3). Through the laying on of hands, God's power would rest on these men, and they were to do great exploits for him.

In the early church when they first chose deacons to help with the duties in the church (so the disciples could give themselves continually to the word of God, as the Bible says), they chose men full of faith and the Holy Ghost whom they then set before the apostles, "and when they had prayed, they laid their hands on them" (see Acts 6). The Bible says that Stephen, one of these deacons upon whom the power and blessing of the Lord rested through the laying on of hands, "did great wonders and miracles among the people" (vs. 8). Here was a deacon fulfilling God's commandments and laying hands on people and seeing great signs and wonders following.

I tell you, the ministry of the laying on of hands is just wonderful!

CHAPTER FOUR

MIGHTY MIRACLES AND HEALING
BY THE LAYING ON OF HANDS

Let us look at the many great miracles and healings that
have been given by God as his mighty power has been
released to people by the laying on of hands. Let's take a
trip together now through some of the New Testament
and find out the things that God did through the ministry
of the laying on of hands. Let's see the POWER flow
through men's hands.

In the book of Mark, chapter 6, verses 2-5,

> *And when the sabbath day was come, he*
> *began to teach in the synagogue: and*
> *many hearing him were astonished, say-*
> *ing, From whence hath this man these*
> *things? and what wisdom is this which is*
> *given unto him, that even such mighty*
> *works are wrought by his hands?*

The Bible tells us that these people did not believe in
this doctrine, so then verse 5 shows the result,

> *And he could there do no mighty work,*
> *save that he LAID HIS HANDS upon a*
> *FEW sick folk, and healed them.*

In Mark, chapter 7, verse 32,

> *And they bring unto him one that was*
> *deaf, and had an impediment in his*

> *speech; and they beseech him to put his*
> *hand upon him.*

Here is a man who is deaf and dumb — couldn't hear and couldn't speak. And the Bible says they beseech Jesus to put his hand upon him — to put his HAND upon him — — TO PUT HIS HAND UPON HIM. Do you get that? And of course, when Jesus put his hand upon him, the healing began to flow into him, and verse 35 says, "And straightway his ears were opened, and the string of his tongue was loosed, and he spake plain." Glory be to God forevermore!

In Mark, chapter 8, verses 22–25, hands were laid upon a blind man. Let's see what happens.

> *And he cometh to Bethsaida; and they*
> *bring a blind man unto him, and besought*
> *him to touch him.*
>
> *And he took the blind man by the*
> *hand, and led him out of the town; and*
> *when he had spit on his eyes, and PUT*
> *HIS HANDS UPON HIM, he asked him if*
> *he saw ought.*
>
> *And he looked up and said, I see men*
> *as trees, walking.*
>
> *After that he PUT HIS HANDS AGAIN*
> *UPON HIS EYES, and made him look up:*
> *and he was restored and saw every man*
> *clearly.*

This blind man received his sight through the doctrine of the laying on of hands. When you obey a doctrine of the New Testament church, you can trust it; you can depend upon it. It will always work. God is obligated to work when we act on his word. The prophet Jeremiah tells us that God watches over his word to perform it (Jer. 1:12). God loves it very much when we take him at his word and do what he says. He then performs the word for us.

In the first chapter of Mark, we have the record of a man who has the incurable disease of leprosy. Do you know of any person who has an incurable disease? Do you have what is called an incurable disease? There is no hope for you? Just read God's word. You will find the hope and help you need:

> *And there came a leper to him, beseeching him, and kneeling down to him, and saying unto him, If thou wilt, thou canst make me clean.*
>
> *And Jesus, moved with compassion, PUT FORTH HIS HAND, AND TOUCHED HIM, and saith unto him, I will; be thou clean. And as soon as he had spoken, immediately the leprosy departed from him, and he was cleansed (vss. 40-42).*

The moment Jesus reached out and touched him with his hand, new skin came on this man. Immediately, the Bible says, the leprosy departed, and the man was completely cleansed. God's POWER flowed through Jesus' hands and drove out the leprosy.

God's POWER flowed through Moses' hands to anoint the leaders of his time.

God's POWER flowed through Paul's hands to heal, to impart the Holy Ghost, to give gifts, to perform miracles; and God's mighty POWER will flow through your hands and sick people will be healed — cripples will walk out of wheel chairs, people will receive the Holy Ghost, miracles will be released from heaven.

Luke 4 shows the POWER in the laying on of Jesus' hands.

> *Now when the sun was setting, all they that had any sick with divers diseases brought them unto him; and he LAID HIS*

> HANDS ON every one of them, and
> healed them (vs. 40).

Isn't that beautiful? He LAID HIS HANDS ON EVERY ONE OF THEM, and EVERY ONE OF THEM WAS HEALED. Every one of our sick folk today should be healed, if they are believers. If Jesus has given this power of his to us, we should be obeying him and laying our hands on sick people. Such needless pain and suffering and torment to the children of God exists. Why don't we just obey God's word and relieve the church of this needless suffering?

There is another dramatic account in Luke 13 of a woman with a spirit of infirmity which the Bible says had her bowed together (bent completely forward) and she was utterly unable to straighten herself or to look upward. That would be pretty terrible, all bent over and not able to help herself. Jesus knew what to do.

> And he laid his hands on her: and im-
> mediately she was made straight, and glo-
> rified God (vs. 13).

Jesus laid his hands upon her. God's Power was released through Jesus' hands and the woman was free and could stand straight and she gave glory to God!

In Acts, chapter 28, verse 8, we find Paul obeying Jesus' command to go into all the world and preach the gospel and teach the things the Holy Spirit had taught him. Paul had been shipwrecked on an island called Melita. He is given hospitality by a man named Publius. Now Paul finds out that Publius' father is sick of a fever. What did Paul do? Did he just wring his hands, as we so often do, and say, "Isn't it terrible! He is sick and suffering so. Dear me, how sad!" No, Paul knew what to do. Jesus had said to lay hands on sick people and they shall recover.

> And it came to pass, that the father of
> Publius lay sick of a fever and of a bloody

> *flux: to whom Paul entered in, and*
> *prayed, and laid his hands on him, and*
> *healed him (vs. 8).*

So, naturally, all the rest of the people on the island heard about it, and verse 9 says,

> *So when this was done, others also, which*
> *had diseases in the island, came, and were*
> *healed . . .*

One time Jesus went to visit Peter, and Peter's wife's mother was sick of a fever. Matthew tells us this story.

> *And he touched her hand, and the fever*
> *left her: and she arose, and ministered*
> *unto them (Matt. 8:15).*

She just rose right up out of the bed and began to minister to the others because God's healing POWER had been imparted into her through Jesus' hands.

Matthew also tells us about a man who had a little daughter who was very sick. You see, your faith can work for your children if you will reach out and touch Jesus and then touch your children. This man said to Jesus,

> *My daughter is even now dead: but come*
> *and lay thy hand upon her, and she shall*
> *live (Matt. 9:18).*

She was so sick, she had actually died. But the man had great faith in the doctrine of the New Testament Church of the laying on of hands, and he continued to believe even though the circumstances looked very bad. The scripture says that Jesus went with him, and so did his disciples. When Jesus got to the man's house, he saw all the people around who were the professional mourners of that day. They would make great mourning noises and play instruments and carry on. Jesus told them that the girl was not dead but she was only asleep. The people mocked and scorned him and did not believe him. The Bible tells us that Jesus put them all out (verse 25)! Jesus got rid of the doubt and unbelief, and he went in himself,

> *and took her by the hand, and the maid*
> *arose (vs. 25).*

The father knew that God's POWER would flow
through Jesus' hands to do whatever was necessary to
help his little daughter, even to raising her from the dead.
The raising of the dead works through the doctrine of the
laying on of hands.

In Matthew 19 Jesus lays his hands on little children.
God loves the little children. He doesn't want them to
suffer and be sick and die before their time. He has pro-
vided the doctrine of the laying on of hands to save the
little children.

> *Suffer little children and forbid them not*
> *to come unto me: for of such is the king-*
> *dom of heaven (vs. 14).*

There is no disease or sickness in heaven.

Jesus doesn't want any disease or sickness to be in
little children. The blessings of God can flow into them
through the laying on of hands.

Have you received the Holy Ghost yet? You can,
through the doctrine of the laying on of hands. Turn to
Acts, chapter 8.

> *Now when the apostles which were at*
> *Jerusalem heard that Samaria had received*
> *the word of God, they sent unto them*
> *Peter and John.*
>
> *Who, when they were come down,*
> *prayed for them, that they might receive*
> *the Holy Ghost: (For as yet he was fallen*
> *upon none of them: only they were bap-*
> *tized in the name of the Lord Jesus) (vss.*
> *14-16).*

You can be saved and baptized and still need to receive
the Holy Ghost. The scripture says they had heard the
word of God and had been baptized, but the Holy Ghost
had not yet fallen upon them.

Read on, verse 17, *Then laid they their HANDS on them, and they received the Holy Ghost.* God's mighty POWER was received by these people through the laying on of hands. This time the power was so great that a man by the name of Simon saw it and wanted to buy this ability to have God's power flow through his hands. Peter severely rebuked Simon for thinking that the gift of God could be purchased with money. No, you can't buy God's blessings. Our money has power to get us the things we want sometimes, but before God all persons are equal — the rich, the poor, the bad, the good, the wise, the ignorant, the prince, the beggar. All God requires for you or me or anyone to receive of his mighty power is for us to love him, serve him with all of our heart and believe. That's all. Mark 11:24 says, "What things soever ye desire, when ye pray, believe that ye receive them and ye shall have them."

Do you need a special miracle? Some folks say that special miracles don't happen anymore. They say that those things died away when the apostles died. That sounds pretty bad for us today, doesn't it? I never could quite understand how people could believe that, though, and still serve a God who starts something he can't finish. He says he is the Alpha and Omega, the beginning and the end, and we haven't come to the "end" yet. In Romans we learn how Abraham felt about God.

> *He staggered not at the promise of God through unbelief; but was strong in faith, giving glory to God: And being fully persuaded that, what he had promised, he was able also to perform (vss. 20,21).*

Oh, let's have the faith of Abraham. Let's believe that if God gives us a promise, he will do what he can do. In Acts, chapter 19, verse 11, it says, "And God wrought special miracles by the hands of Paul . . ." Did you see that word — H A N D S ? If you need a special miracle, it can come to you through the HANDS of a believer. Paul was a believer. God says, if we will lay hands on people, he will release special miracles. If he would do it through Paul, he will do it through you, or he will do it through someone else for you. Sometimes God chooses to do things on his own. But with the doctrine of the church of laying on of hands, you can get that all the time. It will work through anyone's hands — special miracles. Read that over and over.

Special miracles through the hands of Paul. Put your name in there.

Special miracles through the hands of Norvel Hayes.

Special miracles through MY hands — that's YOU!

If you will only believe that God's mighty power will work through men's hands, and if you will lay hands on people in faith, just simple childlike faith, the Spirit and power of God will begin to be imparted to people. Great and mighty works, special miracles will begin to be released to the church through you. Just believe the Bible. Lay hands on people because God said to. He will perform what he has promised to perform.

CHAPTER FIVE

WALK IN THE LIGHT

When you obey the Bible, you are IN God. And when you are in God, you are in the truth. When you are in the New Testament, you are in God.

> *This then is the message which we have heard of him, and declare unto you, that God is light, and in him is no darkness at all (1 John 1:5).*

I mean there is NO DARKNESS AT ALL when you are IN God. God is light and in him is no darkness at all! John goes on,

> *If we say that we have fellowship with him, and walk in darkness, we lie, and do not the truth: But if we walk in the light, as he is in the light, we have fellowship one with another, and the blood of Jesus Christ his Son cleanseth us from all sins (vss. 6,7).*

If we say we have fellowship with God — and most of us would say that we believe in God, we trust in God, we are born again and are now in the family of God, we are really saying we are IN God — the Bible says that if we say we are in God and continue to walk in darkness, we are telling a lie. Either we must walk in the light as he is in the light, or we must quit saying we are in God. One or the other.

We have been showing you all through this book that the laying on of hands is IN God. When you lay hands on people, you release the light to them. The glory of God comes to them IN him in the form of healings, miracles, power of the Holy Ghost, new arms, new legs, new eyes, release from demon power. The light comes. When Jesus was transfigured before Peter, James and John, he shown with such a great light that those fishermen could hardly keep looking at him. He was showing them his glory. He is the light. And if we say we are in Jesus Christ, that we belong to the family of God, we must walk in the light.

> *As ye have therefore received Christ Jesus the Lord, so walk ye in him . . . (Col. 2:6).*

Walk in the light.

Walk in the knowledge of the truth.

Don't let God have to tell you later that you lied, that you said you loved him, but you wouldn't lay your hands on people because you would just let some of the others do that; you weren't sure about it; they didn't do it at your church.

Look at Hosea 4:

> *Because thou has rejected knowledge, I will also reject thee, that thou shalt be no priest to me: seeing thou has forgotten the law of thy God, I will also forget thy children (vs. 6).*

Make sure you don't forget the laws of God. His word, the Bible, is his law! When you obey his word, he does his part, and performs what he promises he will do. But if we do not obey his word, if we do not believe his word, then he says he can't help us. He can't help our children. He must reject us because we have rejected him.

> *In him (Jesus) was life; and the life was the light of men. And the light shineth in darkness; and the darkness comprehended it not . . . He came unto his own, and his own received him not (John 1:4, 5, 11).*

I plead with you, don't say you have received Jesus, and then continue in darkness. If you receive Jesus, take all of him.

> *But as many as received him, to them gave*
> *he power to become the sons of God,*
> *even to them that believe on his name (vs.*
> *12).*

THERE IT IS!

God will release his mighty power through you just the same as he did through his son, Jesus. Because if you receive Jesus, you are also a child of God and to you he gives the power, if you believe on his name.

Can you see it?

CAN YOU SEE IT?

I pray the Lord Jesus Christ will reveal himself to you fully through his Spirit and engraft this word deep into your heart. Receive this light into yourself. Then you can walk in the light and you

> *. . . shall lay hands on the sick, and they*
> *shall recover.*

CHAPTER SIX

LET JESUS TRAIN YOU IN THE DOCTRINE OF LAYING ON OF HANDS

I have gone to church all my life. I saw God's power operate in my church through the ministry of salvation, but I never saw anyone healed. Then when I began to be successful in my businesses, I helped build a large church in my city. By that time we were all so wealthy and so well off, and the church was so big and so full of intellectualism, that I never saw God's power operate anymore at all. Not even enough to speak of in that old time conviction when folks would jump out of their seats and run down to the altar and fall on their faces before God and weep and cry out to God for forgiveness of their sins until the peace of the Lord would come to them. They would weep with joy as their names were written down in the Book of Life.

We would just have an intellectual type sermon, and then after the sermon, we would sing a few verses of *Just As I Am,* and after all that, one or two folks would go down to "join the church."

When God's power is in a place, the scriptures say that sinners cannot stand in the congregation of the righteous (those who obey God). They either have to get out or run to the altar for mercy.

Are sinners comfortable in your church? If they are, are you sure God's power is there? In Romans 13 we have some power-packed verses.

> *Let every soul be subject unto the higher*
> *powers. For there is no power but of*
> *God: the powers that be are ordained of*
> *God. Whosoever therefore resisteth the*
> *power, resisteth the ordinance of God:*
> *and they that resist shall receive to them-*
> *selves damnation (Rom. 13:1, 2).*

Here God is warning us not to resist his power.

I was speaking sometime ago in a Full Gospel Church outside of Philadelphia, and I began to lay my hands on the people who came forth, and set them free from the bondages of the devil. Oh, how sweet it is to watch an operation by the Holy Ghost. Sometimes I have seen God working under their clothes on their bodies. Their clothes rise up around a cancer or some terrible disease that is in their body, and you can see the disease moving around under their clothes, and then all the disease disappears! The cancer would disappear! People who have had diseases fifteen or twenty years are operated on by the Holy Ghost through the laying on of hands and within just a matter of a few minutes are completely healed. The pastor in Philadelphia wanted me to come back and teach for a week. He said, "Norvel, we believe this is God."

Sometimes God puts his power in my hands so strong that my human body almost cannot stand up under it. Sometimes he doesn't. But I don't lay my hands on people because I feel the power in my hands. I lay my hands on people because the Bible says to do it. The power goes into the people whether I feel it or not. You just go ahead and lay hands on people because it is a doctrine of the New Testament Church, regardless of how or what you feel. God will do his part.

You have to be trained to do this if you have been raised in a church that doesn't do it. You probably can pray with someone to receive Jesus because your church believes that and has taught you to do it. But you can also learn to lay your hands on people so God's power can be released to them.

I remember when God began teaching me about this part of his commandments. I had told him I loved him, and he began showing me different things he would like for me to learn to do, like casting out devils and laying my hands on sick people so they would be healed. I am not an apostle, and I do not pastor a large church. I don't even pastor a small church. I am just a businessman that God called to be a disciple, and he said to me, just like he said to the New Testament disciples, "Go ye into all the world, Norvel, go into the parts of the world I tell you to and preach my word, and I will go with you confirming the word with signs following."

If God has called you to be a disciple of his, BE A DISCIPLE.

The word disciple means a learner, so if you are learning about God, then you are a disciple. He will want you to go to certain places and take the gospel to certain people. He will want you to heal the sick,

cleanse the lepers,

raise the dead,

cast out devils (Matthew 10:8) because that is the gospel of the kingdom. We are to teach others what Jesus has taught us. I am teaching you what Jesus taught me.

Now listen closely. Jesus taught me to lay my hands on people. When I went to my large church in a big city, I never saw anybody called forward to be prayed for. I never saw sick people at church have hands laid on them and go home well. I had never seen that. Those who came with coughs and colds and things went back home still with them.

When we moved to Cleveland, Tennessee, God sent a Full Gospel pastor to me. This pastor's name was Reverend Littlefield. He worked with poor children and people who didn't have very much. He came into my office one day and asked me if I would be willing to come to his church and teach a Sunday School class of little poor children whose teacher couldn't be there.

I said, "All right, I'll come," and I went.

I taught the class, and they were the meanest kids I had ever met. I had to put one of them outside so I could teach the class. He was kicking the other kids under the chairs. That was my first experience trying to teach people and finding out that some of them didn't want to learn.

After the class, I decided I would stay for the service. I went upstairs and sat down in the sanctuary. Right when the service started, the Spirit of God fell on me, and the Lord said to me, "I want you to help this man," so for the next few weeks and months, I attended that church from time to time, and gradually Rev. Littlefield began to have me come to the altar with him and help him pray for the people.

I would go to the altar feeling pretty strange because I noticed that they would lay hands on people sometimes. Of course, I didn't do that. Since I was from the First Baptist Church, we didn't do that. Of course, that isn't what the Bible says. The Bible doesn't say you do what the others do that go to your church. Have you ever considered that just maybe your church might be wrong about some things? Your church may be full of men's doctrines and devil doctrines which make the word of God of none effect? My church was.

Jesus let me know real plain one day that he didn't care what they did at the First Baptist Church. He was only interested in what the Bible said. Jesus tried to get me to cast a devil out of a girl one time, and I tried to tell him that they hadn't taught me to do that at my church. He said to me, "The sixteenth chapter of the book of Mark does." And it does!

Now when you first start laying hands on people, your hands feel funny. Reverend Littlefield began to say to me while we would be at the altar, "Put your hands on this person, Norvel, and pray." I would go ahead and do it. I didn't know what I was doing. After he did this to me

two or three times, my hands began to get blessed. I felt
like the bones in my hands were going to jump out. One
night at the altar, my hands were feeling so good, I
walked over to Rev. Littlefield and said, "Reverend
Littlefield, what is happening to my hands? I feel like the
bones are going to jump right out of my hands, they feel
so good."

He said, "That's God's power in your hands. Put your
hands on this person right here. Put your hands on that
person over there, Brother Norvel. Here, Brother Norvel,
put your hands on this person here." God used him to
teach me how to obey the Bible. I noticed that when I
would put my hands on them, sometimes the people
would break and cry. Sometimes they would get healed.
Sometimes they would begin speaking in another language. I said, "Oh, my, Reverend Littlefield, this is wonderful, this is wonderful!"

One day when I was at home, Reverend Littlefield
came up to my house and rang my bell. I went to the
door and he said, "God sent me out here to get you to go
pray for a Methodist woman."

I said, "Well, Reverend Littlefield, why don't you pray
for her?"

He said, "God wants you to go pray for her."

I couldn't figure that out. He was the Full Gospel
Church pastor and I was just a businessman from the
First Baptist Church.

I said, "Do you really think it is God?" I thought
maybe it was just him.

He looked real steady at me and said, "It's God,
Brother Norvel. Jesus sent me out here to get you. He
wants you to go pray for her."

I said, "Well, all right, I'll go. I'll meet you at the
church in thirty minutes."

When I got there I met Rev. Littlefield, and he had his
song leader with him. We bought food and took it with us

to this woman's house. They explained that this woman had three or four children who hadn't had anything to eat because the mother couldn't get up out of bed to fix anything. I thought, "Oh, my, this must be a real tough case."

We all went in, and I noticed quickly that all the dishes were in the sink all dirty. Reverend Littlefield and the song leader fed the little children. Then we went back into the bedroom and there was a woman about thirty years of age in a king-size bed, and she looked like she was dying. She said, "I don't think I ever felt so bad in my life, Reverend Littlefield." He said, "Well, we have come to pray for you."

He told his song leader to go down to the foot of the bed and pray. He said he would kneel down where he was and pray. And he said to me, "Now, Brother Norvel, God wants you to stand up here at the head of the bed and lay your hands on her and pray for her."

I slipped to the head of the bed and began to pray a little prayer, just a gentle prayer, because she was a Methodist woman, you know. The best I can remember, I prayed a prayer something like this:

> *"Now Satan, I break your power over this woman's body, and I command you to let her body go free. Now I thank you, Jesus, for your healing power to go through this woman . . ."*

And here I reached over and gently laid my right hand over her forehead . . .

> *"And I want to thank you, Jesus, for healing her because we do agree and claim the healing power for her body. In Jesus' name."*

My right hand began to turn warm! It felt like a great warm substance was just oozing over and through my right hand and going into her body. She began to quiver.

Her whole body began to shake just a little bit. In sixty seconds it began shaking more. And then more and more.

She said, "Oh, what is this that is happening to me? What is this going through my body?"

I said, "That is the Lord Jesus Christ healing you."

She said, "Oh, yes, oh, yes, I am being healed. It feels so good. Everything is disappearing and I am feeling so good."

Within a matter of just three or four minutes she was completely healed. Her whole countenance was changed. She was turned from a human being who was suffering and moaning and groaning under the burden of the sickness into a person who was filled with joy, with beauty, and feeling good throughout her whole body. With tears streaming down her face and the glory of God all over her, she praised and thanked God. I'm telling you, with the laying on of hands comes the glory and power of God – God's mighty power for his people.

We turned to leave, and I turned around at the door and said, "Well people are supposed to be up and about and doing their work, rejoicing and praising God."

She said, "Yes, that's right. I am healed. I am going to get up. I am going to get up right now."

In about five minutes she came out of that room dressed and ready for work. She walked right over to that sink of dirty dishes and began squirting soap into the sink and washing her dishes, singing and rejoicing, singing songs unto the Lord, and I mean rejoicing so much that we couldn't even hold a conversation with her. We just looked at one another and said, "We might as well get out of here. She is healed and doing her business."

In my car going home I thought, "My, my, Jesus healed her in about two or three minutes, just because I laid my hand on her and prayed."

The laying on of hands is a doctrine of the New Testament Church, and when I laid my right hand on her,

God's mighty power began to flow through my hand into her body, and she was restored back to her family in just a matter of minutes.

She came to Rev. Littlefield's church the following Sunday. I was there. She testified that when her husband came home that night, she told him how she had been healed when the preacher and two other men came to the house that day and laid hands on her and prayed. She said her husband needed to take a trip and all his clothes were dirty and he wanted her to get some washed up for him. Their washing machine had been broken for a while, and her husband meant for her to take the clothes to the laundromat. She testified that she told him, "No, I won't need to do that. If those men can lay hands on me, and Jesus can heal my body, which is a lot more complicated than that old washing machine of ours, he can heal my washing machine. If I just lay hands on it and pray, I know the washing machine will start." You know, when you are full of the glory of God and his power, you can believe for anything!

This little lady went out and put the clothes in the washing machine, laid hands on the machine and prayed. She turned it on, and the water began to come in and the machine began to wash her husband's clothes. He just stood there. He could hardly believe it. She finished her testimony by saying, "So Jesus fixed my body and fixed my washing machine both!"

God has all power in heaven and on earth. If you will just obey him and do things the way he says, you can get most anything done. I'm not telling you to lay hands on your washing machine if it's not working, although if you have the faith to believe God will fix your washing machine, he will. But I am telling you that God will heal sick bodies, every time, any place, all persons. He has established the doctrine of the laying on of hands for the church today.

I know you want to see God's mighty power work for you in the ministry of the laying on of hands. Ask God to have someone begin to teach you like Rev. Littlefield helped me. Or just ask Jesus to continue to teach you what I have taught you in this little book.

Begin today! Don't let any more time go by when needy people are suffering who don't need to suffer, dying who don't need to die, in pain who don't need to be in pain.

God's mighty miracles are imparted to his people in the church today through the doctrine of the laying on of hands.

Do you do it?

When are you going to start?

The sixteenth chapter of the book of Mark says, *They shall lay hands on the sick, and they shall recover.*

Your hands can make the difference between health and sickness.

Your hands can be the difference between power and weakness.

Your hands can make the difference between life and death.

Lay hands on the sick, and they shall recover.

Begin to see the mighty power of God released in your life and in the lives of those you know and come in contact with.

In Jesus' Name,

Amen!

Other Books by Norvel Hayes

*Divine Healing — God's Recipe For
Life and Health*

Worship

Confession Brings Possession

Let Not Your Heart Be Troubled

Endued With Power

How To Live and Not Die

The Winds of God Bring Revival

*God's Power Through
the Laying On of Hands*

The Blessing of Obedience

*Stand in the Gap
for Your Children*

*How to Get
Your Prayers Answered*

*Number One Way
To Fight the Devil*

*Why You Should
Speak in Tongues*

*What Causes Jesus To Work
Miracles?*

*Visions — The Window to the
Supernatural*

Misguided Faith

What To Do for Healing

*Financial Dominion —
How To Take Charge
of Your Finances*

*Rescuing Souls From Hell —
Handbook for
Effective Soulwinning*

How To Cast Out Devils

Radical Christianity

*Secrets To Keeping
Your Faith Strong*

Putting Your Angels To Work

Know Your Enemy

How To Be Led By The Holy Spirit

*Training Camp For
The Army Of God*

The Healing Handbook

Available from your local bookstore.

For additional copies
of this book
in Canada contact:

Word Alive
P. O. Box 670
Niverville, Manitoba
CANADA R0A 1E0